# Table of Contents

Preface .......................................................4

Display of Common Invocation Stances and Poses ...........6

Performing the Magick Circle Consecration Spell .........8

Spell For Centering ......................................11

The Magick Circle Consecration Spell ....................12

A Spell For Opening the Summoning Circle ................15

A Spell for Sacrifice ...................................16

An Invocation to a Binding Union ........................19

An Invocation for a Physical Manifestation ..............20

A Spell for Binding .....................................23

A Spell for Self-Sacrifice ..............................24

A Pledge of Service .....................................27

A Pledge of Submission ..................................28

An Invocation For Guidance and Protection ...............31

A Plea for Safety .......................................32

An Invocation for An Instruction ........................35

A Plea for Guidance .....................................36

An Spell for Protection from Hostile Influences .........39

A Reflection and a Request ..............................40

An Spell For Success & Acceptance of Consequences .......42

An Spell for Success, Health, and Wealth ................45

An Spell for Power ......................................46

An Spell for Charisma ...................................49

An Spell for Strength ...................................50

An Spell for Terrifying Fierceness ......................53

An Spell for Triumph Over One's Adversaries .............54

An Spell For Rapture ...................................57

A Plea for Guidance ...................................58

A Powerful Reminder of Faithful Service .................61

Praises for Blessings ...................................62

Releasing the Deity/Spirit ...........................65

## PREFACE

The study and practice of magick (an an alternative spelling of magic that emphasizes magick as a more studied/scholarly enterprise and practice) can easily become one of your most fulfilling and wonderful experiences! With a fuller understanding of both the traditional and occult nature of things, you'll find yourself capable of having a significant impact on your environment.

Now let's turn to the meaning of "black magick"maintained by this book. Foremost, I do not promote nor recommend using these spells to invoke demonic powers. In my understanding, "black magic" differs "white magic" since it is resolutely self-centered. Using white magic, our focus is on aligning with - and hopefully positively - influencing the Universe, in a manner favorable to us. That is, we seek the best outcome for ourselves and others.

If you're interested in this application on magick, you might also be interested in my book, **Magic Spells for Manifestation and Protection.** That being said, I did have fun creating more sinister artwork for you to enjoy with this project :)

To make my spells more accommodating to the world's many beliefs and religions, I've put a blank line during the opening invocation for you to personalize with your preferred deity/ entity.

Next to increase your skill and further your appreciation of how a multitude of outside factors can affect the outcome of your spells, I recommend you devote serious effect to mindfully journaling and accurately logging your spell casting. If this interests you, check out **Moon Magic Log Tracker | A Guided Journal for Spell-casters.**

# DISPLAY OF COMMON INVOCATION STANCES AND POSES

Below are illustrations of common poses assumed during ceremonial magick. Use these as reference points and adjust as necessary to adopt the form that best suits you. You may assume multiple stances during your spell work, and should allow your intuition to guide your movements.

# PERFORMING THE MAGICK CIRCLE CONSECRATION SPELL

1. Draw a circle on the floor around your alter for protection against hostile forces. Be certain to make it large enough for you to assume your invocation pose(s) without allowing your extended arms, legs, or body to extend beyond the confines of your circle.

2. Approximately 3, 6, or 9 ft from your protection circle, draw apart another for the deity/spirit summoned approximately 3 feet in diameter.

3. Light a black candle on your alter, and say the Spell for Centering.

4. Dress in all black and drape yourself with a black cloth or wear a black, hooded robe.

5. Light sticks of incense: myrrh, frankincense, and sandalwood.

6. Assume your chosen invocation pose.

7. Holding the incense sticks, say the Magic Circle Consecration spell.

8. Say your chosen spell.

9. State your intention(s)/desire(s) – no more than three. You may also write them on paper and burn them using the flame from the black candle.

10. Release the spell binding the entity.

11. Light a stick of sage incense or smudge stick. Say a spell for protection.

12. Carefully stick your foot outside of circle. If you have ANY sense of foreboding or negative energy, do not attempt to leave the circle! Let the incense burn for approximately 5 minutes, and then try again. If the hostile energy remains,

summon the entity again to request assistance in expelling the hostile force(s).

13. Turn on a fan, open a window or door(s) and walk slowly throughout the space with the sage incense/smudge stick until it the energy feels properly balanced.

## SPELL FOR CENTERING

O [insert name of deity],
Spring open my heart and mind's gate!
I invoke the power to influence this my fate
With all the strength of my will.
Let the threads of fate be stilled.
Now, banish all other thought.
My will focus firmly on what is now sought!
[State your intention.]
I impel you, [deity], to grant this to me.
As I will, let it be! (3x)

## THE MAGICK CIRCLE CONSECRATION SPELL

Ascending with the power of both dark and light
I harness the powers of the night,
Against hostile forces now set a ward –
Let this magick circle be my guard
O [insert name of deity]!
See my sacrifice.
Hear my plea.
Come and reveal thyself to me!
[Deity/Spirit's Name] grant the request I bring now to thee.
I impel you, [deity], to grant this to me.
As I will, let it be! (3x)

## A SPELL FOR OPENING THE SUMMONING CIRCLE

O [insert name of deity],
Pour thy secrets and ways in me beyond the brim.
My hesitation and anxiety throttle and stem.
Reveal your power through this text's lines.
Reveal what's needed for us to bind
And I'll bind us ever so tight.
I will happily serve you in exchange for your might.
I impel you, [deity], to grant this to me.
As I will, let it be! (3x)

## A SPELL FOR SACRIFICE

O [insert name of deity],
For thy aid in this sacred space,
I offer thee this sacrifice in this place.
My heart, mind, and possessions I did scour
For sacrifice in exchange for your power.
I invoke the powers of three,
Bow my head, and bend the knee.
I offer this and myself to thee.
Wash thy mystic powers over me,
And forever your servant I will be.
I impel you, [deity], to grant this to me.
As I will, let it be! (3x)

## AN INVOCATION TO A BINDING UNION

O [insert name of deity],

I beseech you to take me as you vessel.

Bring me close, my being please nestle.

Your awesome power makes me gasp.

Seize me now with your fearsome grasp.

I request an awe-inspiring wisdom,

And the resources to build my own earthly kingdom.

If need be, to you I'll be fettered

If it'll bring me something even greater.

As I will, so let it be.

Grant your power unto me.

I impel you, [deity], to grant this to me.

As I will, let it be! (3x)

## AN INVOCATION FOR A PHYSICAL MANIFESTATION

O [insert name of deity],
Come to me now in your pure and mystical form,
For I invoke thee now against hardship's storm
Use thy power both light and dark
to place me on destiny's most favored arc.
Reveal to me the cost of what I ask.
What must I do to make my fortunes last?
I impel you, [deity], to grant this to me.
As I will, let it be! (3x)

## A SPELL FOR BINDING

O [insert name of deity],
Before our union, I was bruised and tossed by
fate's vicious storms and bitting winds.
My sole yearning was for the pain to end.
With your intervention, may I continue
to know certainty and peace.
Grant me such and I sacrifices and service will not cease.
O [deity], let thy mysterious power be mine!
In this magick ceremony, I do us bind.
I impel you, [deity], to grant this to me.
As I will, let it be! (3x)

## A SPELL FOR SELF-SACRIFICE

O [insert name of deity],
I relinquished my soul
In the pursuit of the things to make me whole
I seek a satisfaction so deep and profound
A desire to which I'm utterly bound
I invoke such a powerful, immortal **force**
To put me on success' inexorable course
It truly will never my being disturb
If I accumulate more than I deserve
I impel you, [deity], to grant this to me.
As I will, let it be! (3x)

## A PLEDGE OF SERVICE

O [insert name of deity],
I'm prepared to do whatever you do deign.
I love you dearly and would be loved fain.
Forever bound, we are of one mind.
And willingly so! I'm glad to be thine.
There is no questioning my devotion to thee:
You've consumed my essence entirely.
I impel you, [deity], to bestow your favor on me.
As I will, let it be! (3x)

## A PLEDGE OF SUBMISSION

O [insert name of deity],
Our covenant remains ever on my mind.
My fortune and soul now so entwined.
Dedicated and ascendant, I'm ready for
whatever next is in store.
I've seen and felt your power & ask that you share more.
Thank you for such wondrous pleasures you've granted to me!
Guide me to wherever I need to be.
I impel you, [deity], to grant this to me.
As I will, let it be! (3x

## AN INVOCATION FOR GUIDANCE AND PROTECTION

O [insert name of deity],

Grant me access to more than that's allowed

Swallow me in your protective shroud

For in your power, I have no doubt

I invoke your name and amazing things come about.

Guide me true, and guide me far

What a fearsome duo we are!

I impel you, [deity], to grant this to me.

As I will, let it be! (3x)

## A PLEA FOR SAFETY

O [insert name of deity],

My pain I pray you see that I offer thyself to thee.

Deem not thy sacrifices less

I stand before you in the utmost humbleness.

In your armor I pray thyself shod.

Cleanse my soul most beautiful God,

In the midst of these spells,

Grasp my soul and secure it in your unbreakable snare.

For if you do,

These self-centered spells you'll guide me through.

I pray these doings take my to heavy a toll

On my immortal soul.

I impel you, [deity], to grant this to me.

As I will, let it be! (3x)

## AN INVOCATION FOR AN INSTRUCTION

O [insert name of deity],

Teach me thy ways, doctrine, and ancient truths;

I properly submit my appeals to you:

As my immense desire aches and grows;

So you improve my position by your throes!

I praise you to skies above.

Make me worthy of your attention, favor, and your love!

I impel you, [deity], to grant this to me.

As I will, let it be! (3x)

## A PLEA FOR GUIDANCE

O [insert name of deity],
In the midst of these spells,
Grasp my soul and secure it in your unbreakable snare,
For if you do,
These self-centered spells you'll guide me through.
Reveal to me the cost of this toll,
and how to properly perform my role.
I impel you, [deity], to grant this to me.
As I will, let it be! (3x)

## AN SPELL FOR PROTECTION FROM HOSTILE INFLUENCES

O [insert name of deity],

My pain and desire, I beseech you to see,

And accept what I now offer thyself to thee.

Deem not these sacrifices minor nor less,

I stand before you in the utmost humbleness.

In your armor I pray thyself shod.

Cleanse and protect my soul most beautiful God.

I impel you, [deity], to grant this to me.

As I will, let it be! (3x)

## A REFLECTION AND A REQUEST

O [insert name of deity],

Consecrated now, and sacrificed whole.

So did I promise my very soul.

What was the true cost of its worth?

And what did it unleash upon this vicious earth?

Did I give enough thought - take an adequate pause?

Did I fully consider the consequences it'd cause?

Enough I considered when I pledged myself to thee,

Now [insert name of deity], grant what you promised me.

I impel you, [deity], to grant this to me.

As I will, let it be! (3x)

## AN SPELL FOR SUCCESS & ACCEPTANCE OF CONSEQUENCES

O [insert name of deity],

I beseech thee for an impressive domain:

Establish a formidable kingdom in my name,

Steel me now for consequences of this campaign,

And Ensure that all my enemies are incapacitated and slain.

Through all hardship, my reign sustain

And your humble servant I shall remain

I will be strong and now soberly acquiesce

To whatever sacrifices are necessary for my success

I impel you, [deity], to grant this to me.

As I will, let it be! (3x)

## AN SPELL FOR SUCCESS, HEALTH, AND WEALTH

O [insert name of deity],
Look favorably on all I bring to this mystic fire.
For higher and higher still, I burn with desire
Coalesce, fulfill, strengthen the roots of all my things,
Let me be amazing, fearless, and a well from which success,
health, and great wealth springs.
I ache for this deeply - down to my very bones,
I pray to claim an awesome throne,
And a majesty all my own,
I beg, I plead, and I pray to be the best.
Eager to do whatever and leave to you the rest.
I impel you, [deity], to grant this to me.
As I will, let it be! (3x)

## AN SPELL FOR POWER

O [insert name of deity],
Fulfill my needs, let me feel no dearth
Grant me the pure ecstasy in this  earth
No mere change, I desire a complete rebirth!
I invoke splendor as wide as the open sky.
I pray you grant this and more to I.
For greater things do I pine.
Grant this to me - let all this and more be mine!
I impel you, [deity], to grant this to me.
As I will, let it be! (3x)

## AN SPELL FOR CHARISMA

O [insert name of deity],

I ask lips of honey and quickness of thought

To exploit fully the things our magick hath wrought

The source of my fortune, I may not choose tell;

But this I know, and know full well,

Within thy might, my soul now dwells

I, your servant, am under your spell,

I impel you, [deity], to grant this to me.

As I will, let it be! (3x)

## AN SPELL FOR STRENGTH

O [insert name of deity],
I invoke the strength to handle whatever I come upon.
Dispel all my troubles and lead me on.
I embrace my future and wisdom from my past.
Take me to you now and hold me fast.
Within you, fashion me anew.
My soul, I entrust to you.
I impel you, [deity], to grant this to me.
As I will, let it be! (3x)

## AN SPELL FOR TERRIFYING FIERCENESS

O [insert name of deity],

Not a mere semblance, but in thyself true power

Fill me now and make it flower

All we have willed, hoped or dreamed shall exist;

Grant me signs so that I may steadily persist

For unto you am I bound

and so unyielding - utterly terrifying - on my battlegrounds.

Let my adversaries cries fill the sky;

So powerful soon shall be I.

I impel you, [deity], to grant this to me.

As I will, let it be! (3x)

## AN SPELL FOR TRIUMPH OVER ONE'S ADVERSARIES

O [insert name of deity],

My spirit soars, my enemies lurk,

Let them be bound tightly and not affect my work.

O [insert name of deity], hear my heartfelt praise!

Come within me now and instruct me in your ways!

For my ultimate triumph, mold me to your design.

Grant me all things I desire to make mine!

Man, brute, temptress - whichever suits my aim,

I request your divine assistance by invoking your Name.

I impel you, [deity], to grant this to me.

As I will, let it be! (3x)

## AN SPELL FOR RAPTURE

O [insert name of deity],

Take me to you for I

So that I may sit contently on high

I conquer and I rend

The depths I'm willing to reach, few can comprehend

Make my enemies quiver and shake

As everything from them I take.

Grant me power and endless majesty,

As I will, so let it be.

I impel you, [deity], to grant this to me.

As I will, let it be! (3x)

## A PLEA FOR GUIDANCE

O [insert name of deity] what have I not said?

I stand before you humbly - I quickly bow my head.

Have my thanks come too slow?

I've feverishly sought and praised you as you well know.

Speak to me now, your silence I both loathe and fear.

My sacrifices have been and ever are so sincere

Before me now, you must appear

You said you'd heed my call and right now I invoke you here.

I impel you, [deity], to grant this to me.

As I will, let it be! (3x)

## A POWERFUL REMINDER OF FAITHFUL SERVICE

O [insert name of deity],
Never I dithered nor never agonized
Over the sacrifices deemed necessary for my prize.
My lust, my grace, my dreams, and my fears –
I'll relinquish much of what I previously held dear
Raise me up, free from others' schemes and woes.
Steady my rise through these ebbs and flows.
As a humble servant unto thee,
I impel you, [deity], to grant this to me.
As I will, let it be! (3x)

## PRAISES FOR BLESSINGS

O [insert name of deity],
By the light of this magick flame,
I now invoke your ineffable name!
Builder and maker of fortunes with your sacred hands.
Wishing I can feel your power steadily expand.
I impel you, [deity], to grant this to me.
As I will, let it be! (3x)

## RELEASING THE DEITY/SPIRIT

O [insert name of deity],
I give you my thanks, and release you gratefully back.
May this binding between us grow slack.
Your power and wisdom, I do pray to keep near,
And hope my future calls you hear.
My guide and my might, I bid you farewell;
So, I release you with this spell.
I impel you, [deity], to grant this to me.
As I will, let it be! (3x)